Soul Hydration

Soul Hydration

How to satisfy your spiritual thirst with the living water of the Holy Spirit

Dr. Linda A. Day

First Paperback Edition 2023
Printed in the United States of America
ISBN: 979-8-218-19609-7
www.drlindaday.com

COPYRIGHT NOTICE

The self-assessments in this book are provided for informational purposes only. They should not be used to replace the specialized training and professional judgment of a medical health care or mental health care professional. Neither the author, the editor, nor the publisher is engaged in providing medical or mental health professional advice in this book. Readers should consult competent professionals before using any information/suggestions in this book.

Neither the author nor the publisher can be held responsible for the reader's use of the information provided within this book. The reader should always consult a trained professional before treating themselves or others.

Unless otherwise noted, scripture quotations are from the King James Version of the Bible. King James Bible. (2017). King James Bible Online. https://www.kingjamesbibleonline.org.

Published by Dr. Linda A. Day – drlindaday.com.

Book Cover Design, Interior Design, Editing, & Graphics:
Tara L. Culton | virtualsolutionswithtlc.com

Ordering information: Email info@drlindaday.com.

Table of Contents

FOREWARD

Dr. Linda Day is extending an open invitation to explore the realities of true healing. Healing when you do not realize you need it or will not acknowledge it. Healing from the well of the Lord.

In this book, Dr. Day calls life situations challenges, Samaria experiences, distractions, detours, and valleys. She provokes your mind and spirit to have a real encounter with life situations via the Samaritan woman's story. Embark on your journey with zeal. This book will stir your emotions and stretch them in new ways.

Life has thrown you a curve ball. There are perpetual challenges to your faith. And you are stretched beyond what you believe you can bear. These are the times when you feel empty, unfruitful, and thirsty. These situations are what Dr. Day had in mind when she wrote this book. And she encourages you to drink from the well that never runs dry. Jesus.

Elder Nancine Dreon

"If we want greater clarity in our purpose or deeper and more meaningful spiritual lives, vulnerability is the path."
Brené Brown – Research Professor at the University of Houston
(Brown, n.d.)

Vulnerability is what we've been missing. In this society, unfortunately, we have been taught that vulnerability is a bad thing. It is not. In this manuscript, Dr. Day opens the word of the Lord using the Samaritan woman as a model. More importantly, she opens herself as an example. She is vulnerable.

In these pages, Dr. Day shares intimate moments and powerful illustrations from her life. Openly. Honestly. Truthfully. I know because I have watched her live out some of them. She shows us instances of having a 'dehydrated' soul. She shows us what it is like to have a soul needing hydration through her story. Dr. Day then shows us why we shouldn't live that way. She indicates that there is a remedy for your thirst.

Please do more than read this book. Digest it. Selah. Pause and reflect. Next, receive the revelation that God is downloading to you for you. If you do this consistently, you can rest assured that Jesus will quench your thirst, and the rivers of living water within you will flow again. He, alone, is the remedy for a soul that is dried. He, alone, can provide soul hydration.

Tara Culton, Peer Recovery Specialist
Mental Health Coach
Creator | Talks with Tara C: Healing Conversations About Mental Illness
NAMI State Trainer – (National Alliance on Mental Illness)
NAMI IOOV (In Our Own Voice) Presenter
NAMI Peer-to-Peer Facilitator
NAMI Connections Facilitator
Owner – Virtual Solutions with TLC (Executive Virtual Support)

DEDICATION

First and foremost, I dedicate this book to my Lord and Savior, Jesus Christ, who is the source of spiritual nourishment and hope. May he fill every page with His presence and with His grace. Amen.

I dedicate this book to the spiritually dehydrated, mature single woman who has a heart for God but struggles with loneliness and extreme thirstiness (intense cravings for something or someone other than God). This book is an escort, leading you to the river of God, where spiritual hydration awaits. He will save you through His Word and rejoice over you with joy.

May God bless all who read this book. May it quench your spiritual thirst and cause you to be spiritually hydrated and full of hope.

"The LORD thy God in the midst of thee is mighty;
he will save, he will rejoice over thee with joy;
He will rest in his love, he will joy over thee with singing."
Zephaniah 3:17 KJV

ACKNOWLEDGMENTS

Special thanks go out to my legacy. They are my son, Larry Bailey, Jr; my daughter-in-law, Ashley; my son, Lorenzo A. Bailey; my grandchildren, Desmond, Arianna, Porcia, Zavier, and Zaahir. And our newest addition, Hendrix.

Each one of you is the joy of my heart. Words cannot explain how I feel when I look at you. I am truly a blessed woman, Mom, "DD," Nanna, Gigi, and Grandma Linda.

To my spiritual parents, Bishop Daniel Robertson Jr. and Co-Pastor Elena Robertson; my mentor Dr. Pamela J. Downing; Elder Nancie Dreon. My co-laborers of the gospel, Elder Tara Culton, Minister Erna Seaberry, and Elder Angelic Brown, thanks for pushing me even when I did not want to be pushed.

To my Mt. Gilead Full Gospel International Ministry family (Richmond, VA), I love you guys.

Rehydrating my soul with you,
Dr. Linda A. Day

"I consider my life worth nothing to me, if only
I may complete the task the Lord has given me."
Acts 20:24

PREFACE

This book will transform your life - more than just giving you more information. At the end of each section, I have created space for a 'Selah moment.' It is a place to stop and ponder on what you have read. Please look deep within and listen closely. You will find that God is speaking to you in unique ways. You will also recognize the place from which your thirst originates.

Write what you sense, feel, and hear the Father saying. This data will prove beneficial as you walk towards God's river for soul hydration.

This book is about the Samaritan woman and her thirst. Her thirst was not from natural sources but from a dry place within her. I use her as your sacred guide to show you the various types of thirstiness, where they may have originated, and what to do now. Knowing this is important because to fulfill your God-ordained destiny, you must recognize that staying spiritually dehydrated positions you to miss God's best for your life.

Three things happened that are significant to the Samaritan woman's story (and yours too):

- She meets her Savior.
- She recognizes she's a sinner, which causes her to repent.
- She becomes an evangelist (she told others about her encounter).

Remarkable! The Jews and Samaritans were not bosom buddies. More about that later. So, the fact that Jesus even spoke to her was a miracle. She acknowledged that in John 4:9.
But then again, it IS Jesus. (In Nehemiah 6, you can read how this strained relationship between the Jews and Samaritans started.)

This book is also about you.

As you read this book, I pray it is more than informative. I desire it to be transformational and full of revelation. I want you to examine how a trip to the well (Jesus) can transform, refresh, revitalize, and rejuvenate your soul when you are spiritually thirsty. We need to understand why our souls are spiritually dehydrated and, more importantly, how to prevent soul dehydration in the first place.

The Samaritan woman's story explores how spiritual thirst reflects our need for God and why spiritual dehydration keeps us from experiencing God's best for our lives. Ultimately, through her story and mine, you will learn to be a spiritual responder and seek the spiritual refreshment Jesus offers. We need Soul Hydration.

"The spiritual did not come first, but the natural, and after that the spiritual."
I Corinthians 14:46

INTRODUCTION

Sometimes, you come to a crossroads where you find yourself stuck and repeatedly go around the same mountains. I know I did. In my heart, I knew there had to be something better, so after being sick and tired of being sick and tired, I made a conscious effort to pause, reflect, and analyze my life.

I recognized that my habitual mistakes were all due to how I saw myself and that I looked for validation from people, especially men, much like the Samaritan woman *(John 6:4-30)*. I had finally found the root of my problem. Now I was ready to move forward and fill that void with spiritual affirmations that came from speaking the word of God over myself. I was prepared to go to the well where I would find the essential nutrient I needed, Jesus, the living water.

I knew I needed Soul Hydration.

To be sure, there are untold numbers of women who were or are where I was. They are women in their mid-life who have completed raising their children, retired from their careers, and are single. They love the Lord and are active members of their local congregations. But their souls are dehydrated because of loneliness, loss of identity, and lack of Godly companionship.

I call the place I was in (and many women like me) Samaria. It is a place of hills and valleys. Samaria is a place where strongholds can capture you. It is a place of desperation, boredom, sadness, madness, and fearfulness. These emotional triggers had me watching my life move in a downward spiral.

Although I know and love Jesus, somehow, I let myself believe there was no hope until I made a trip to the 'well.'

I discovered that Jesus had been waiting for me at the well during those times!

The book you have in your hands uses the Samaritan woman's life loosely as an example. I will share parts of my story, and, of course, I will talk about Jesus' story. A little bit. (I say a little bit because there are not enough pages to write about Him.)

Who is she – this Samaritan woman? And what do we have in common with her?

We meet the Samaritan woman at a physical well. For our purposes here, the well will serve as a metaphor to describe a place of deliverance. A well is any place where you surrender, repent of your sins, and receive Christ as Savior. John the Baptist, Jesus' cousin, eloquently said, *"Repent for the kingdom of heaven is at hand." Matthew 3:2 (KJV)*

The Samaritan woman went to the well to draw water. Because of that act, her life changed forever. She had an encounter with Jesus. Remarkable! Why? Because the Jews and Samaritans were not bosom buddies. The Samaritans were part Jewish and part Gentile. And neither group wanted to associate with them. So, the fact that Jesus even spoke to her was a miracle. She acknowledged that in *John 4:9 (KJV).*

Jesus' presence at this well was not a coincidence or accident.

Why did the Father send him? It was an assignment to rescue God's daughter from a life of bondage. Can you identify with that?

I can.

There were many areas of bondage in my life. I was so used to things being as they were that I did not recognize the consequences of my rash decisions as bondage.

When we make hasty decisions, we could go down a destructive path. We have to be led by something other than our emotions, beliefs, and desires, which often can lead us to make hasty decisions. We must first recognize our need for the Savior and surrender ourselves to His will. We must come face to face with our sinfulness and acknowledge that our decision-making process has ultimately led us to the brink of destruction. We must confess our wrongs and repent, turning away from a life of sin and towards Jesus Christ, who can fill the void in our lives.

Much like the Samaritan woman at the well, it is only then that we can become true evangelists, sharing our testimony of redemption with others and leading them away from the unhealthy paths their decisions could take them down. That's how this book came into existence. Jesus rehydrated my soul. Now I want to tell others about the need for soul hydration and its benefits.

We make bad choices. We are not bad people.

It is important to remember that while we may make bad choices, it doesn't mean we are doomed. We have a Savior willing to forgive us and help us make better life decisions. We don't have to stay stuck in the cycles of unhealthy decision-making – we can strive for transformation through Him.

No matter how dire our situation may seem, if we turn to Jesus Christ and rely on Him for guidance, he will always lead us down far better paths than any hasty and unhealthy decision we could make. It is one of the most heroic things you can do when you decide to turn away from your sinful nature and seek after Christ. And by doing so, we demonstrate our faith in Him and open ourselves up to a life full of joy and purpose. We must remain steadfast in our faith, trusting God to make everything possible.

I wrote this book as a guide to help mature faith-based women go 'back to the well.' Women like me. We worship beautifully and enthusiastically on Sundays, Wednesdays, or whatever day your faith group meets. Then a lot of us go home to an empty home. Often it is in that space where we make decisions that are not good for us. Why do we do this?

We do this because we have allowed our souls to become dry. We may only gather with other like-minded people during Sunday worship, Bible study on Wednesdays, choir rehearsal, etc. And we believe we are okay until we realize that something is amiss. All too often, we need help to identify what is missing.

We need a trip back to the well.

The Samaritan woman's story gives us hope. I hope we can have the same experience if we are willing to go to the well to receive soul hydration.

HOW TO USE THIS BOOK

This book is meant to be revelatory. It is written to help reveal why your soul needs hydration and how you got to that point. It is not for information purposes only. You can get information from any internet search.

This manuscript is designed to cause you to pause and reflect truthfully on where you are in your spiritual life. Selah Moments. To stop and remember what the Lord has called you to do. And to identify the barriers that keep you from getting there.

You will see provocative questions for you to answer. There are also worksheets and self-assessments to help you along the way. Use them to support you as you allow the Holy Spirit to minister. In these vulnerable areas, you can dig deep and partner with God. He is patiently waiting for you to come to the well. He knows you need Soul Hydration.

Use the Scripture Focus sections to listen to God's heart about you. Let the scripture presented uncover the Father's love for you and fill you with what you truly need. If God puts a different scripture on your heart, follow His leading

PART ONE - WHAT IS IT?

DEHYDRATION vs. HYDRATION

WHAT IS SPIRITUAL DEHYDRATION?

Before we go any further, let us clarify what I mean by spiritual dehydration. Spiritual dehydration occurs when you lack the proper moisture level (Jesus' living water) deep down in your spirit and life. As a result, you may do whatever you believe is necessary to quench that thirst. That may be getting involved in destructive relationships, spending too much money, using drugs, etc. All these behaviors are just symptoms of the problem. They point to a need for God, His word, and the power of the Holy Spirit.

The Bible says first the natural, then the spiritual. "Thirst is a defense mechanism," states Matthew Goldman, MD (Cleveland Clinic, 2022). It is like that in the spirit realm. Your spirit may be crying out to tell you something is missing. That missing ingredient is vital to your everyday life and helps you reach your Kingdom destiny. It is the Lord. It is the water of His word.

Knowing the symptoms of soul dehydration is critical in helping you identify when you are getting spiritually thirsty. This dehydration will cause you to veer off the Kingdom course God has for your life.

- Extreme loneliness. This symptom signals that you may have forgotten that you are never alone. In this state, you may make unwise decisions for companionship. The enemy of your soul knows this. He sends in counterfeits that fill that void for a while. Or so you think. My sister, you are never alone. Keep *Matthew 28:20* in mind, *"...And behold, I am with you always..."*

- Spiritual dry mouth. This symptom reveals itself when you have negated to feast on the word of God (living water) and dwell in His presence. You may have also failed to declare, decree, and give back to the Lord His word. Speaking to the Samaritan woman at the well, Jesus said, *"If you knew the gift of God, and who it is who says to you, 'Give me a drink,' you would have asked Him, and he would have given you living water." John 4:10*

- Fatigue. Not only must you speak the word of the Lord, but you also have to ingest it. Without daily ingesting God's word, you will get tired and overwhelmed. Your energy is drained because you are trying to live your life devoid of God and the direction he gives in the Bible. Jesus had something to say about this in *John 14:6*. He said, "*I am the way and the truth and the life. No one comes to the Father except through me.*"

- Boredom. The symptoms come alongside loneliness. When you are bored, alcohol, drugs, or sex may seem like excitement and the answer to boredom. However, these habits, and others, are tough to break.

WHAT IS SOUL HYDRATION?

So many people are physically dehydrated but don't know it. And so it is in the spirit realm. Soul dehydration starts long before you are aware of it.

We are so accustomed to doing what we want when and how we want to do it. In general, we have stopped spending quality time with God. Consequently, these are some of the symptoms we experience spiritual heart palpitations (fear):

- Inability to eliminate effectively (release our cares and concerns to God)
- Tiredness (we keep going around and around the same set of circumstances)
- Confusion (we are not hearing the Father's voice with clarity)
- Overheating (we allow our emotions to lead us)

All of this causes spiritual dehydration. Just like physical dehydration, this is dangerous to our spiritual health. If we are not careful, we can find ourselves:

- Having a heart attack (emotional distress caused by any number of circumstances)
- Being constipated (the inability to heal from hurts)
- Feeling weary (no energy to fight the attacks of the enemy)

- In turmoil (a constant state of mental distress over life's challenges)
- Lacking self-control

We can define hydration as reinstating the water that we lost. Hydration also involves the body's capacity to receive and retain water. As children of God, we understand that water symbolizes the Holy Spirit. So, here is our working definition of soul hydration:

> *Reinstating the Holy Spirit to His rightful place in our lives by having intimate time with the Father, ingesting the Word of God, and executing God's commands.*

I will call life situations, challenges, distractions, detours, and valleys in this book. These situations will disrupt your spiritual development and destiny. They will also guide you to receiving soul hydration. How? By putting God back on the throne of your heart.

Tackling your spiritual thirst head-on is crucial. You are already in a spiritual deficit when you recognize that you need soul hydration. Hydration with the word of God is required. The living water must flow into your life again to rehydrate you properly.

Keeping the spiritual disciplines of prayer, fasting, journaling, reading the Bible, and meditating on scriptures are pivotal in keeping your soul hydrated. These disciplines will also help build a hedge of protection all around you.

Let me ask you this "What have you been doing in your life? Have you been feasting on television, social media, gossip, dwelling in the past?" Whatever it is, be intentional about spending time in God's word. This daily habit will help you make decisions that move you forward on your path to destiny.

YOU ARE THIRSTY, BUT YOU WON'T DRINK

We all make excuses to justify sin. We know when someone is not suitable for us. We all desire to be loved but often settle for less than what God has for us, and then we wonder why we are all tangled up in sin. God is a gentleman who will not oppose what you want because he allows us to choose right from wrong. He gives us free will; it is His grace and mercy but not a ticket to blatantly sin.

"It is of the LORD's mercies that we are not consumed, because his compassions fail not. They are new every morning: great is thy faithfulness." Lamentations 3:22-23

Soul hydration comes with freedom. But to be free, you must first want to be free. The Merriam-Webster online dictionary offers one definition of free as "not bound, confined, or detained by force." When you lack soul hydration, you are bound by your thoughts, confined by your actions, and detained from reaching your destiny. You are in a wrestling match.

What you have been wrestling with in your quest to be free has nothing to do with flesh but is the spirit realm of ranking rulers that are out to destroy you:

"For we wrestle not against flesh and blood, but against principalities, against powers, against the rulers of the darkness of this world, against spiritual wickedness in high places." Ephesians 6:12 (KJV)

It is not the individual who has you under control but the spirit of the "strongman" (demonic presence) who has come and set up a defensive structure in your life to keep you bound. Therefore, it is critical to get to the root of this strongman and destroy him:

"How can one enter into a strong man's house and spoil his goods, except he first binds the strong man." Matthew 12:29

Release the power of God on the situation:

"Verily I say unto you, Whatsoever ye shall bind on earth shall be bound in heaven: and whatsoever ye shall loose on earth shall be loosed in heaven." Matthew 18:18

From the website of Kimberly Snyder:

What Is A Strongman Spirit?

"A strongman spirit is a high-ranking principality spirit. They sit on thrones in the spirit realm and rule over the evil demonic spirits that operate in the earth realm. These spirits can rule over certain

> *geographical areas of the earth. Strongman spirits can operate in churches as a ruling spirit. They can be passed down through family generations and also dwell within an individual. We must always remember that our fight happens in the spirit realm. Our fight is not against people. Our battle is against principalities, powers, the rulers of the darkness of this world and against spiritual wickedness in high places. These are the demonic spirit forces that have set up thrones in the second heaven to block to our prayers to God and from receiving our answers. These forces block our prayers, our deliverance and our freedom."* (Snyder, 2023)

Even though you are in church and love the Lord, you are not exempt from bondage. I know. I was there.

When you need soul hydration, you separate yourself from Jesus. The longer you stay disconnected from Jesus, the more the hole and empty feeling within will grow. It will get larger and larger until it consumes you to the point where you will always seek temporary things to fill that void.
How do I know this?

I always sought other things and people to fill what only Jesus can. The moment I surrendered and allowed Jesus to be captain of my soul was when my life changed dramatically. If you want to learn who Jesus is and how you can take his word and incorporate it into your life, you must immerse yourself in the word of God. The time is now for you to find out what God desires of you. The time is now for you to grow your faith. Great treasures wait for you as you reengage in your relationship with God.

THE THRILL IS GONE

Growing up in New York, my mom and dad would have parties. An often-played record was an album by B.B. King called "Thrill is Gone" (Hawkins & Darnell, n.d.) Some of the lyrics to the song are:

"You know I'm free, free now, baby
I'm free. Free from your spell
I'm free, free, free now
I'm free from your spell
And now that it's all over

All I can do is wish you well."

Essentially, he said I am moving from this relationship to another because this one has gone wrong, and I am no longer fascinated and influenced by you. I can relate to this song because there was a time in my life when I was in and out of relationships, losing my integrity and dignity, and just along for the ride to hear someone tell me, "I love you."

We have an innate desire to be loved. Sometimes we will go to any length to receive love. When we do that, we are spiritually dehydrated.

Often, I think about all the relationships in which I was involved. The thrill was gone. But because I needed love, I wanted love, and I desired love, I would straddle the fence in many areas of my life. This was especially true regarding my relationship with Jesus. I have since learned that when you are a child of God, you are royalty, a daughter of Zion, or a mighty man of God. You are part of the royal priesthood. You deserve only the best. Nothing less. Scrambling, scratching, and 'doing whatever it takes' to get love is not who you are. Everyone is not worthy of your affection.

God does not want you to be second best to anyone, especially if they don't treat you with dignity and respect. More importantly, if they are not in a covenant relationship with Jesus like you are, you need to step back and reassess the situation before you get so deep into it that you are spinning around. Without Jesus at the center of your relationship, it is doomed before it even starts. Trust me. I have learned the hard way about entering relationships where both of us have excess baggage from past relationships into our relationship (actually, any baggage is extra).

The world is always searching for true love. That does not exist in the context of what we think is true love. The world's standard and definition for "true love" is having a solid and lasting affection for someone while being happy and passionate about that person. The Greek term theophilia means the love or favor of God. (Wikimedia Foundation, 2023) *I John 4:16* says:

"And so we know and rely on the love God has for us. God is love. Whoever lives in love lives in God, and God in them."

It is God's love that we need. I am referring to God's love for his creation, which is "agape." Agape love is unconditional and the highest form of love.

The word of God tells us that Jesus came so that we might have life and have it more abundantly. How can you have this abundant life when you are tangled up in bondage to things and people? And more importantly, you are disconnected from Jesus, the bread and source of life. He is the living water – the only one who can hydrate your soul.

In the natural realm, you need food for nourishment and growth. The same concept applies to the spirit needing spiritual nourishment to sustain your spiritual growth. We are lost and need to be saved, and only Jesus can save us:

"That if thou shalt confess with the mouth the Lord Jesus, and shalt believe in thine heart that God hath raised him from the dead, thou shall be saved." Romans 10:9

Only with Jesus can you find hope, peace, joy, and hydration for your soul. When trials and tribulations come (and they will), you can move forward knowing Jesus is right at your side:

"And there is a friend that sticketh closer than a brother." Proverbs 18:24

Selah moment- for those with older brothers, you should be able to identify with a big brother coming to your assistance when the neighborhood bully was picking on you. The gospel's good news is that Jesus is our big brother, and big brothers take care of their siblings.

SOUL HYDRATING ACTIVITIES

SELAH MOMENT – Hydrating Your Soul

Time for Soul Hydration

PREPARATION IS KEY

Your soul stays hydrated when you prepare. Your soul will stay spiritually hydrated when you are consistent with the activities below. Make sure to add specific steps (6-8) and actions that the Holy Spirit gives you.

"Thou wilt keep him in perfect peace, whose mind is stayed on thee: because he trusteth in thee." Isaiah 26:3

STEPS	ACTIVITY	SCRIPTURE	DONE? Y or N
1	Quiet Time, Soaking	Psalm 16:11, John 4:24, Psalm 46:10	Y or N
2	Prayer	Matthew 17:20, Isaiah 59:1, Psalm 37:23, Luke 5:16	
3	Journaling your conversations with God	Habakkuk 2:2	
4	Study the Word of God	2 Timothy 2:15	
5	Put the word in action	John 13:17, James 1:22-25, James 2:18	
6.			
7.			
8.			

SELAH MOMENT – Hydration for Your Soul

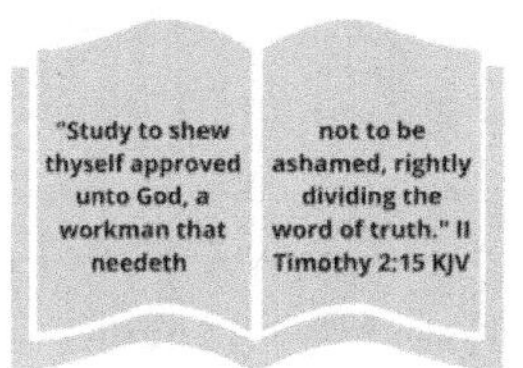

SCRIPTURE FOCUS

Use the scripture below or one that speaks to where you are on your 'soul hydration' journey right now. What is God saying to you through this scripture? What is keeping you from believing what Jesus is saying to you? Be honest.

"But whoever drinks of the water that I will give him will never be thirsty again. The water that I will give him will become in him a spring of water welling up to eternal life." John 4:14

YOUR DAILY 'WATER' INTAKE – Gratefulness

MAKE COPIES AS NEEDED

On your calendar, create your usual daily schedule. Notice if your schedule is jammed packed or not. When we are accustomed to being busy all the time, we often neglect those things that quench our thirst. Things such as quality time with God. Time with family and friends. Your alone time. Time to engage in activities you enjoy. These are important to maintaining your inner 'water levels.'

What are you grateful for right now?

Below, list things for which you are grateful. Then take a moment to Selah. Pause and reflect on areas of growth that will prevent spiritual dehydration.

____
____
____
____
____
____
____
____
____
____
____
____
____
____
____
____
____
____
____
____
____

YOUR DAILY 'WATER' INTAKE

Natural Realm

To-Do
I must plan my day for my soul and body's hydration

MAKE COPIES AS NEEDED

Use this to craft your daily schedule and be intentional about your time with the Father. Also, be sure to get enough natural water too!

EXAMPLE SCHEDULE	Natural Water Intake
6:00 AM Intimate time with God	For each glass of water you have, check it off here. Each circle represents an 8oz glass of water.
7:00 AM Prepare for work	❍ ❍ ❍ ❍ ❍ ❍ ❍ ❍ ❍
8:00 AM Drive to work	❍ ❍ ❍ ❍ ❍ ❍ ❍ ❍ ❍
9:00 AM Work	❍ ❍ ❍ ❍ ❍ ❍ ❍ ❍ ❍
10:00 AM	❍ ❍ ❍ ❍ ❍ ❍ ❍ ❍ ❍
11:00 AM	❍ ❍ ❍ ❍ ❍ ❍ ❍ ❍ ❍
12:00 PM	❍ ❍ ❍ ❍ ❍ ❍ ❍ ❍ ❍
1:00 PM	
2:00 PM	
3:00 PM	
4:00 PM	
5:00 PM	
6:00 PM	
7:00 PM Bible Study	

SPIRITUAL HYDRATION SCHEDULE
What will you do today to quench your inner thirst? Plan specific times during the day to 'refill.' Schedule those times here. Put a checkmark when completed. Think of things like meditating on the word, praying, reading the word, etc.
1.
2.
3.
4.
5.
6.

SELAH MOMENT – Goals

MAKE COPIES AS NEEDED

Every Kingdom daughter (and son) should have goals. Goals help you focus and accomplish God's will for your life. They are your roadmap. Ask God to reveal what he wants your life to look like. Use the space below to identify and document your progress toward your goals. Only focus on three goals during this time. (You can always make copies of this sheet as you set new goals.)

Goal #1: Did I achieve it? Why or why not?

Goal #2: Did I achieve it? Why or Why not?

Goal #3: Did I achieve it? Why or Why not?

PART TWO - THE PROBLEM

"Ask yourself a most profound question:
"What are the two most important days in my life?"
The day you were born and the day you realize why you were born!
And why were you born?
You were born to bless the lives of others.
You were born to make a contribution." (Canfield, 2016) [1]

"The Samaritan woman grasped what He said with fervor that came from an awareness of her real need. The transaction was fascinating. She came with a bucket. He sent her back with a spring of living water. She had come as a reject. He sent her back being accepted by God Himself. She came wounded. He sent her back whole. She came laden with questions. He sent her back as a source for answers. She came living a life of quiet desperation. She ran back overflowing with hope. The disciples missed it all. It was lunchtime for them."
Ravi Zacharias (Zacharias, n.d.)

[1] The base of this quote has been frequently attributed to Mark Twain. However, after extensive research, I found that the quote as written above, was created by Anita Canfield in her book, A Woman and Her Self-Esteem. 1985, A Woman and Her Self-Esteem by Anita Canfield, Quote Page 43, Randall Book Co., Salt Lake City, Utah. (Verified on paper)

THE VOIDS

Have you ever been so thirsty that nothing eliminated that parched, dry feeling regardless of what you drank? It could be water, lemonade, iced tea, or soda. You kept searching for something that would quench your thirst. Continuously searching for something to fill a void is how life can sometimes be.

When you are empty inside, the desire to seal that void will cause you to try things that are temporary pleasures for the moment. When the thrill is gone, you start the process again, searching for that one thing. Consequently, your search for wholeness leads to temporary satisfaction and even more aridness.

The void we may be trying to fill might be loneliness, depression, feelings of lack, unworthiness, the need for attention, or several other reasons. We know that something is missing. We know we deserve more. But we don't know how to go about being fulfilled. Our souls are dry and barren.

When I speak of the soul, I am talking about your mind, will, and emotions. The three parts that constitute who you are. It is your spirit. This part of you, your soul, creates the problem of spiritual dehydration. Consequently, you seek 'refreshment' wherever you can find it. Perhaps you desperately want companionship. Or do you desire authentic friendships that help propel your Kingdom purpose? Do distractions sidetrack you and block forward movement on your road to destiny?

Your mind may make you think you are complete only when you are in a relationship or when a man gives you attention. Your will causes you to make decisions outside of God's best for your life. And emotions? Your emotions can be everywhere.

When you are in a spiritual drought, you can be happy, sad, angry, jealous, and in turmoil. You get where this is going.

Let me give you an example of how this plays out.

ATTENTION SEEKING

My late ex-husband was an alcoholic. I met him while on tour when I was in the army. How did we meet? We met because I was high. Okay. Let me back up.

I enlisted in the army because I wanted something more than what I was experiencing in my life after graduating from college. One tour took me to Germany. Berlin, to be exact. I went out with a friend one night, and, unbeknownst to me, her boyfriend was THE drug dealer on the base. They were drinking and smoking. I didn't want to be the party pooper. I also did not want to be excluded from the so-called 'fun.' So, I drank what they had.

I also smoked what they had. I had no idea that what I was smoking was laced with hallucinogens. That's right. The type of drugs that cause people to disassociate and hallucinate. I knew something was wrong. However, I was powerless to help myself. Know what happened? They took me outside the club, leaving me on a bench. Alone. In the dark. In a country where I knew no one. I sat there for quite a while. Then, my soon-to-be husband and some other soldiers saw me. They were kind enough to help me by walking me all night! Then they escorted me back to my apartment.

Talk about God's saving power!

I had no idea about having a call on my life. And it was apparent that I surely was not heeding that call even if I did have an idea about it. Nevertheless, God had angels on assignment. Indeed *Romans 8:28* was in effect.

> *"And we know that all things work together for good to them that love God, to them who are the called according to his purpose."*

Do you see how desperate I was for attention? I almost lost my life to be a part of the 'in' crowd. The reality is that I wanted to be loved and accepted. This acceptance was something I was missing in my younger years.

THE ROOT

Today I stand as a proud African American woman. That was not always the case. When I was a child, the children would bully me because I had dark skin. They would call me ugly, black, and all sorts of names. Frequently I could be found sitting or playing alone. I was an outcast.

Because of being treated this way, the root of my low self-esteem dug and trench in my spirit. This trench became a void I unconsciously tried to fill in various ways. The most prevalent manifestation was seeking the attention and approval of men.

MOISTURE DEPRAVATION

After divorcing my late ex-husband, I rededicated my life to God. I was on fire for the Lord. That is until the day someone from my past resurfaced. The enemy knows what you desire and will present it with bows, bells, and whistles. Before I knew it, I was straddling the fence, trying to serve God and be in the world simultaneously. The flesh will always want to be entertained, and yes, it feels good, but once it's over, condemnation sets in.

Oh, sure. I still went to church. Faithfully. However, I wasn't faithful to God. I thought everyone was looking at me with judgmental attitudes and cynicism. As a result, I sat in the back with my head down. One Sunday, my Bishop, Daniel Robertson, Jr., said something to the effect of "...someone has reentered your life; they are no good for you. Leave them alone!" I wanted to melt through the floor.

I decided to call it off but fell back into my old ways when I saw him that afternoon. Why? Because I wanted the attention, he tickled my ear with his seducing words. Before he resurfaced, I had been working on a project but put it aside for an entire year. He was a distraction, and I knew it, but I was not as strong then as I am today.

COVENANT BREAKING

There was a time when I would have affairs with married men. They had to be married because I did not want a commitment. That stemmed from past trauma. I knew the men would eventually have to go home to their wives.

My college science teacher was my first voyage into adultery. His wife was a professor at the college. Please don't judge me.

This man was part of the Kappa Alpha Psi fraternity and was immensely popular. Not only was he popular, but he was a very handsome man. Many of the ladies in the school had an eye for him. Somehow, I caught his attention. Thinking I had it going on with this older man, I would meet him on side streets, and we would head down to some of my family members' homes, about fifty miles from the school, to spend time together.

When school was out in the summertime, I would stay in Alabama instead of returning to New York. Often, I would ride to the campus to see him. This craziness lasted the entire four years I was at the college. Do I feel bad? Of course. At the time, I did not care, nor was I aware that he did not meet my emotional needs. There was no security, community connection, no real validation, etc. It was all physical.

I also did not understand how impactful the decision to commit adultery would have on my life later. It was the beginning of a cycle of mistrusting men. It was also a trap for me in emotional affairs with men. (We'll leave that for another book.) Years later, I repented for my sins when I came to know Jesus. Although I did not ask for forgiveness from his wife face-to-face, I did ask God to forgive me for being a part of breaking the marriage covenant.

Attention-seeking is trying to take God's glory. Why do I say that? Because you want to be the focus. You want to be the apple of someone's eye. Attention-seeking is a sure sign that your soul needs hydration. Seek God's blessings instead.

SOUL HYDRATING ACTIVITIES

SELAH MOMENT – Spiritual Dry Mouth

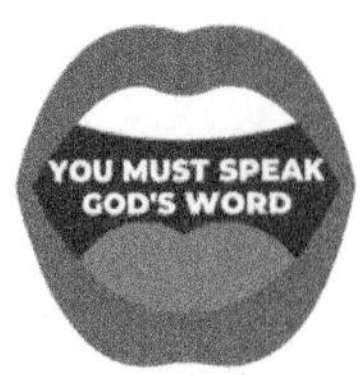

In the space below, write about when you first noticed you were not saturated with God's presence. Did something happen that became more of a priority than God? How does that make you feel? What do you want to do about it?

"You make known to me the path of life; in your presence, there is fullness of joy; at your right hand are pleasures forevermore." Psalm 16:11 ESV

SELAH MOMENT – Attention Seeking

"Study to shew thyself approved unto God, a workman that needeth not to be ashamed, rightly dividing the word of truth." II Timothy 2:15 KJV

SCRIPTURE FOCUS

Use the scripture below or one that speaks to where you are on your 'soul hydration' journey right now. What is God saying to you through this scripture? What is keeping you from believing what Jesus is saying to you? Be honest.

"But unto them that are contentious, and do not obey the truth, but obey unrighteousness, indignation and wrath." Romans 2:8

SELAH MOMENT – Desperate for Attention

Recall times in your life when you were desperate for attention. You may have been seeking attention from a particular person, your family, friends, coworkers, faith community, or whomever. Don't be hard on yourself. Don't judge what you write. Just write it down for now. Write as long as it takes to get everything out.

"Watch this: God's eye is on those who respect him, the ones who are looking for his love. He's ready to come to their rescue in bad times." Psalm 33:18-22 (MSG)

SELF-ASSESSMENT – Self-Esteem

Sometimes our self-esteem is at the root of our spiritual thirst. That's because we have not properly viewed ourselves from God's perspective.

Take this self-assessment below to determine if your self-esteem needs to be elevated.

This self-assessment is for you. There is no scale, grading, etc. Allow the Holy Spirit to reveal to you the areas he wants you to work on.

1. When I am feeling dry and parched or unfulfilled, I go to the word of God:
    a. Always
    b. Sometimes
    c. Never
    d. I have no idea.

2. Good self-esteem helps you to have what around others.
    a. Confidence
    b. Optimism
    c. Mood swings
    d. Self-concept

3. Having a positive attitude towards your future means that you are:
    a. Resilient
    b. Vibing
    c. Optimistic
    d. Confident

4. Self-awareness includes knowing about my:
    a. Strengths
    b. Weaknesses
    c. Hobbies
    d. All of the above

5. What is a need?
    a. A boat
    b. Flowers
    c. Food
    d. Clothes

PREPARE YOUR TESTIMONY

What is a testimony? A testimony is your declaration of how you have come to know God in a real, personal way. It is your statement of how you have seen Him work in your life.

Has he healed you? Transformed you? Rescued you? Put the broken pieces of your life back together? Whatever he has done, it's time to start crafting your testimony so that you will not have the diagnosis of spiritual dry mouth.

Write out how you were a broken vessel in the streets hooked on drugs, committing fornication, adultery, drinking, and partying for years, or whatever your testimony is. Share how you were in hell because of your lifestyle but did not know. Then one day, an encounter with Jesus changed all that, and you have not been the same.

Things to consider:

- The day you got saved.
- What was your life like before you met Jesus (or recommitted your life to him)?
- What were the consequences of your decisions before Jesus?
- Although you are saved/recommitted to Christ, there may be consequences of past behavior. How do you handle that?
- How did you handle your emotions before? What about now?
- How did you handle the topic of forgiveness/unforgiveness?
- What were your thoughts about money? What are they now?
- Can you share about maintaining the tithe?
- If asked, could you explain the Trinity?

PREPARE YOUR TESTIMONY

PREPARE YOUR TESTIMONY

THE CHALLENGES

CHALLENGES CAN DEHYDRATE YOUR SOUL

SAMARIA CHALLENGES

The word "challenge" can be described as something you face that requires your full attention (mentally, emotionally, spiritually, financially, or physically) so that the result is successful. No matter how much it hurts, go through the process. Refrain from trying to figure out how you are coming out. Just know you will.

"The Lord orders the steps of a good man." Psalm 37:23

"Samaria" is derived from the Hebrew word Shome-ron, meaning "a watch-mountain or a watchtower." (M.G. Easton M.A., n.d.) All of us are responsible for actively 'watching' over our lives. But many don't. Instead of actively 'watching' and engaging, they allow life to go by lackadaisically. They have no enthusiasm to participate in life at all passionately. The only thing they watch is their life going by. They are used to their daily routines.

Some of the routine daily activities include taking the kids to practice, going to work, taking the same driving routes, coming home, watching television, playing on the game boxes, and then going to bed. No wonder people feel empty inside, and the zeal and zest for life are no longer there. This repetitive lifestyle is the beginning of spiritual dehydration. They are busy, bored, and broken.

Recognize challenges as brief distractions and pivotal learning experiences that can positively or negatively affect our souls. It all depends on how we embrace the moment. In either case, there were two options. I encourage you to deal with the challenges. If you don't, they will become repeated lessons to learn. Many would not have known who God is if it were not for the challenges.

Some of the challenges we go through, we cause them, and God allows them. At other times they come from the enemy who comes to sift you like wheat *(Luke 22:31-34)*.

WORLDWIDE CHALLENGES

During the pandemic, governments worldwide mandated that people stay home for extended periods. Brick-and-mortar houses of worship closed (before beginning online services). This inability to move around caused stress for the old and the young on many levels. Many found themselves facing challenges they never anticipated. These challenges threw them for a loop. Many have not fully recovered. And they are spiritually dehydrated on many levels.

On a worldwide scale, the pandemic was undoubtedly a challenge. The world came to a standstill. Many businesses closed – some for good. Death, and the grief accompanying it, were unlike anything seen in the last 100 years or so. A disruption in the family routine resulted in increased mental health condition diagnoses. The pandemic created food shortages and supply chain disruptions.

These disruptions and shortages had a profound impact on the lives of everyone. The stress, anxiety, and despair resulting from the pandemic are still present with us today. And to cope with the effects of the pandemic, many turned to things other than God. Turning away from God leads to spiritual dehydration.

Challenges were not part of God's original plan for our lives. Still, they are pivotal learning experiences – even living through the pandemic. Depending on how we embrace the challenges, they can be positive or negative. Either way, there are only two options: deal with them, or they will deal with you.

PERSONAL CHALLENGES

Challenges can influence one's mind to ask, "Does God really exist?" Know this. If you have a challenge going on in your life, the enemy of your soul will take those challenges, blow them up, and make them more significant than they are. Nevertheless, if not for the challenges, many would not have learned who God is.

"It was good for me to be afflicted so that I might learn your decrees." Psalm 119:71

What you have been through, or are going through, will not destroy you but will strengthen you. While you are going through it, maintain your joy. Let me remind you,

"Peace I leave with you, my peace I give you: not as the world giveth, give I unto you. Let not your heart be troubled, neither let it be afraid." John 14:27
and

"These things I have spoken unto you, that my joy might remain in you, and that your joy might be full." John 15:11

As Christians, we have something the world does not have that continuously hydrates our souls. We have peace within, whereas the world deals with external feelings that give temporary joy but won't last. In his letter to the Church of Philippians, Paul tells them the secret of joy is found in the Lord, no matter how dark the challenge may be. You grow with spiritual challenges. And having a soul that is fully hydrated ensures you can overcome them. Afterward, you can reevaluate life from a different perspective.

Challenges do not come as hardships alone. They can come in the form of temptations that cause you to sin. (Remember my story?)

The challenges you go through are not new to God, just unknown to you before you faced them. God's word tells us,

"All things work together for good to them that love God." Romans 8:28

There is nothing that you go through that is a surprise to God. He allows it for his glory. So, stop complaining and go through the challenge. You will be victorious at the end of your race because Jesus' death on the cross has paid the price.

The challenges and situations I have gone through did not destroy me; instead, they made me stronger. I kept my joy, and my soul was hydrated because I was ingesting the word of God. God said,

"Count it all joy when ye fall into divers' temptations." James 1:2

"Peace I leave with you, my peace I give you: not as the world giveth, give I unto you. Let not your heart be troubled, neither let it be afraid." John 14:2

"I kept my joy because the word of God reminded me that God would never leave me nor forsake me (Hebrews 13:5) because he was my refuge and strength and ever-present help in trouble." Psalm 46:1-3

"These things I have spoken unto you, that my joy might remain and that your joy might be full." John 15: 11

"Fear thou not; for I am with thee: be not dismayed; for I am thy God: I will strengthen thee; yea, I will help thee; yea, I will uphold thee with the right hand of my righteousness." Isaiah 41:10

I immersed myself in God's word because that kept me from falling apart. I did not understand what was happening, but I knew everything was working for my good. There is no place to which God's knowledge and power do not extend—even in my mishaps and challenges. God has it all under control.

LESSONS ABOUT CHALLENGES

THE SAMARITAN WOMAN

Jesus' earthly ministry was about doing the will of his Father. He would always say he was about his Father's business. When Jesus was about 12 years old, traveling with his family to Jerusalem for Passover, he stayed behind. Mary, his mother, did not notice he was missing until she got home. She checked with other family members, but no one saw him, so she returned to Jerusalem and found him in the temple with the priests. Today was no different. He was on a divine appointment. On this day, two lives would cross, and destiny would occur.

The Father had sent his son to correct some things in his daughter's life. This meeting was not random; God planned to show Jesus' love for us through Jesus' encounter with the Samaritan woman. Nothing that happens in our lives is a coincidence; everything is strategically in motion for a specific purpose and time, and if you are in the wrong place at the wrong time, you will miss your divine appointment. On this day, the woman from Samaria went to the well to draw water as usual, or so she thought. Before Jesus went to Samaria, he had gone from town to town, performing miracles, healing people from all types of sickness and disease, and spreading the good news.

Traveling all day, in addition to the sun being hot during this time of day (noon), Jesus was tired because he was operating in a human capacity. He needed to rest. I believe that if the disciples had been with him, they would have prevented the encounter with Jesus. In this culture, men usually did not speak to women, much less a Samaritan woman. The Bible does not say how long time had passed before this woman came to draw water. But we do know one thing. Nothing could have prepared her for what was about to happen.

Because of the Samaritan woman's lifestyle, she came during the hottest time of the day because the town people (read church folks) probably ostracized her. Society has a habit of judging people, and we are so quick to forget at one time we were lost too. This judgmental spirit is prevalent today in our society and, sadly, in our churches.

Even though the church is supposed to be a hospital for the sick, we turn people away because they do not look, act, or even smell like us. Who are we to judge? You do not know their story. Remember, we all have a story to tell. This judgmental spirit causes many witness opportunities to be lost. The Message Bible puts it this way:

"Don't pick on people, jump on their failures, criticize their faults—unless, of course, you want the same treatment. Don't condemn those who are down; that hardness can boomerang. Be easy on people; you'll find life a lot easier. Give away your life; you'll find life given back, but not merely given back—given back with bonus and blessing. Giving, not getting, is the way. Generosity begets generosity." Luke 6:37-38 MSG

What's the challenge?

The first challenge for us as a Kingdom community of people is to embrace people, provide guidance and encouragement, and show them the direction to Jesus. Let's snatch them from the hands of the enemy. We don't know about other relationships the Samaritan woman may have had. But I believe it is safe to say that she was an outcast. People judged her because she had so many husbands and was shacking up with another man. Because of the culture, people were more than likely very judgmental. How does that apply to us?

The next time you want to be judgmental, remember where you were before you met Jesus. Upon arriving at the well, I am sure the Samaritan woman was quite surprised to see someone sitting there, especially a man who, from his physical appearance, was not from the area. She knew he was different because he spoke to her, something the other town folks did not do. She would soon discover that her past was not about to dictate her future. Jesus met her in her sin, just as he met us in our sin. The Bible tells us we all have sinned and fallen short of the glory of God *(Romans 3:23)*

When you are judgmental, arrogant, and full of pride, that is a clue that you need soul hydration.

And think about this. Many of us believe we can never encounter Jesus because of our past. When you are at your weakest point, Jesus will meet you right where you are. He knows what you need and when you need it. The Samaritan woman had no idea she was empty inside until Jesus revealed her life story. Before meeting Jesus at the well, this woman was spiritually dehydrated. She was in a dark place that had her gripped, and the only thing that could lose her was the redemptive power of Jesus. In all her brokenness and emptiness, she received genuine love and a spiritual flow that would continue after she left the well.

"For he has rescued us from the kingdom of darkness and transferred us into the kingdom of his dear Son." Colossians 1:13 (KJV)

THE ISRAELITES

If we are to learn from any group of people in the Bible who went through challenges, it would be the Israelites. God chose them and led them on a journey to the Promised Land. They had specific instructions and directions. On departing from Egypt, they complained they did not have enough food *(Exodus 16:1-13)*. God sent them bread from heaven (manna) that tasted like honey. He sent it daily. And they were instructed to gather just enough for that day's provision. The seventh day was rest. He told them to pick enough manna for two days, and for evening meals, he sent quail.

All God wanted was obedience and trust in Him. He requires that of us today despite challenges. Not just for our salvation but for the direction of our lives *(Proverbs 3:5-6)*. God had already proven himself and his love for them by the many miracles he performed on their behalf. Nevertheless, they were stubborn and wanted what they wanted. Does that ring familiar to you?

ESTHER

Let's take a look at Queen Esther's life. You can read her full story in the Book of Esther. I'm giving you the synoptic version.

First off, being a queen was never on her radar. She was Jewish. She was an orphan. And she was raised by her cousin, Mordecai. Her path to queendom began after King Xerxes dismissed Queen Vashti because Queen Vashti would not flaunt her beauty as he requested. (I'm paraphrasing.).

Then, after being chosen to enter what some would call a beauty pageant, Esther becomes the new queen. But the story progresses.

One evening Mordecai overheard a plot to kill the King. He told Esther about it and asked her to tell the King. She did. As a result of this, the would-be assassins were hanged.

Now the King's right-hand man, Haman, was full of pride. He wanted everyone to bow down before him. But Mordecai would not. That made Haman extremely angry. Consequently, he wanted Mordecai dead and made plans to have him hanged. Haman was incensed that Mordecai was a Jew on top of him not bowing down. So, Haman made plans to have all of the Jews killed.

The plot thickens.

Mordecai goes to Esther to tell her what is to take place. He pleads with her to go before the King. In those days, you did not just roll up on the King. If you had not been summoned and gone before him, the King could have killed you immediately. What was she to do?

Esther proclaimed a three-day fast. After the fast, she went before the King. Because the King was enamored of her, he extended his scepter. She got what she wanted – a banquet with Haman present. Little did Haman know that she was about to expose him! And she did just that. Again, I encourage you to read the full story in the Book of Esther.

What's the challenge?

Esther endured challenges on various levels. She was:

- a young woman taken from the only home she knew and thrust into the limelight.
- a Jewish woman in the King's palace
    - Her identity had to remain hidden if she was to survive.
    - There were few people whom she could trust.
- marked for death by Haman because of her ethnicity.
- forced to grow up fast, overcome fear, and do what was necessary.

"Go, gather together all the Jews that are present in Shusha, and fast ye for me, and neither eat nor drink three days, night or day: I also and my maidens will fast likewise; and so will I go in unto the king, which is not according to the law: and if I perish, I perish." Esther 4:16

How would you like to be in Esther's shoes? She, like most of us, did not expect to face the challenges she faced. I cannot imagine what it was like for her to go from having no responsibilities or very few to making life-saving decisions for herself and others. Regardless of all that, she moved forward, relying on the mighty hand of God. We should do the same.

DEBORAH

You can find Deborah's story in the Book of *Judges 4*.

The prophetess and judge, Deborah, was all too familiar with Israel's downfall. Because of this familiarity, Prophetess Deborah ruled and reigned from a place of strength. She heard God clearly and executed what she heard as God commanded.

One day, the Lord led her to tell Barak, a commander, that God wanted him to gather a volunteer army and war against the Canaanite warrior, Sisera. But there was a problem. Sisera had a reputation for being vicious in battle. Furthermore, Sisera's troops would outnumber Barak's by a long shot. Sisera could, at that time, overpower almost anyone's army. Nevertheless, Deborah delivered the message. Deborah also let Barak know how she would help him conquer Sisera.

Barak was not convinced at all. He was so afraid of Sisera. Deborah said (paraphrased), "Alright. We will do it your way. I will go with you and be beside you instead of waiting for you. But believe me. You will not be the one to take Sisera out. He will die by the hand of a woman."

What's the challenge?

These are some of the same challenges that women face today:

- Deborah was a woman. Women were looked down upon and not taken seriously. She led at a time when being a woman military leader was unthinkable.
- Deborah had no equal. She did not have contemporaries to whom she could turn for advice.
- Deborah led a people who had lost faith in God.

Imagine the questions that may have run through Deborah's mind:

- "Am I good enough?"
- "Will the people respect me?"
- "Who can I trust?"

These had to be some of the questions. Perhaps Deborah could have asked:

- Will my position in ministry (prophetess) keep me from having a fulfilling relationship?
- As a judge and prophetess, I've had great success on the battlefield. Who can I share that with?
- Will life always be like this?

Sure. I'm taking a creative license here. But you can certainly see how those questions could come up. Even so, Deborah did not negate her Kingdom-responsibility as a judge. Nor did she skimp on any word/instruction that God gave her. Hers was a life sold out for God and whatever his desire for her life was.

Let us all be like Deborah. She kept her soul hydrated with God's word – literally. (There was not a King James Bible in those days!). She paid attention to the details of the instructions the Lord gave her. And she was obedient even in the face of challenges.

We could learn a lot from her.

Unfortunately, life challenges are unlike tornadoes and hurricanes, where you have advance notice to prepare for them. Newly converted saints (new babes or babes) in Christ believe that when they receive salvation, all life's challenges will go away. I am here to inform you that no one is exempt from facing challenges.

"A righteous man may have many troubles, but the Lord delivers them from them all." Psalm 34:19

and

"Indeed, all do desire to live godly in Christ Jesus will be persecuted." 2 Timothy 3:12

Challenges do not necessarily mean hardships. They can come as temptations that can cause you to sin. Whatever kind of sin you allow to enter your life, God hates it. He is holy, and everything that surrounds him must be holy. Sin results from people wanting to roll with the devil and live for God simultaneously. You cannot have it both ways. You must decide. God gave you free will. He also allowed you to choose between life and death, blessings and cures *(Deuteronomy 30:19).*

The Christian journey can be compared to a race where people start strong, believing they will make it to the finish line. But when trouble or pressure presents itself, they crumble because they require soul hydration.

Move out of the way during those troubling times and let God work the situation out. Stop trying to fix everything in your strength. Contrary to what you think or have been told, this Christian journey is not complicated, strict, or rigid. However, it requires obedience regardless of what is going on in your life.

People will ask you, "Why is this journey so hard and complicated?" or "Is this Jesus stuff for a select few?" To them, it appears that everyone else is getting blessed, and they are still waiting.

"Beloved, think it not strange concerning the fiery trial which is to try you, as though some strange thing happened unto you: But rejoice, inasmuch as ye are partakers of Christ's sufferings; that, when his glory shall be revealed, ye may be glad also with exceeding joy If ye be reproached for the name of Christ, happy are ye; for the spirit of glory and of God resteth upon you: on their part he is evil spoken of, but on your part he is glorified." I Peter 4:12-14

SOUL HYDRATING ACTIVITIES

SELAH MOMENT – Drink Up!

SCRIPTURE FOCUS
Now that you know your container (Spirit Man) must fill up daily, grab your 'spiritual gas can' and describe what you are hearing, feeling, and sensing.

Be as detailed as possible so that you can begin to recognize when your soul needs rehydrating.

"For he satisfieth the longing soul, and filleth the hungry soul with goodness." Psalm 107:9

SELAH MOMENT – Accept the Challenge

STAND ON GOD'S WORD NO MATTER WHAT YOU GO THROUGH

SCRIPTURE FOCUS

God loves you so much. He also knows you. He is confident in your ability to master any challenge you may face. The question is, "Will you accept the challenge?"

Meditate on the scripture below. Then write down what the Holy Spirit is revealing to you. Think about what you have already overcome as a springboard to give you peace for any future trouble you may face.

"Blessed is the man that endureth temptation: for when he is tried, he shall receive the crown of life, which the Lord hath promised to them that love him." *James 1:12*

SELAH MOMENT – What's Your Challenge?

DESTINY DESTROYING DEPENDENCIES

ADDICTIONS

Today, many people are addicted to many things, such as drugs, pornography, food, cars, men, women, and money (the list can go on). If they are not careful, that very thing will become their idol. Idol means "a person or thing that is greatly admired, loved, or revered.) (The Britannica Dictionary, 2023). The word 'addicted' implies the inability to stop using/doing/engaging in something that causes harm.

In other words, something has consumed them to the point where they cannot think or do anything other than have the desire to spend all their valuable time centered around this behavior or activity. And because of the addiction to this thing, they neglect their responsibilities and relationships. Unfortunately, many people do not recognize or see the red flags of addiction before them until it's too late. By then, they have lost their families, money, dignity, self-respect, etc.

So now they are stuck in this black hole, thinking that there is no hope of ever coming out, and in their minds, they are convinced nothing will change. You are right; nothing will change if you do not do something about the situation.

The enemy has convinced many people that what they are dipping and dabbling in is not a sin, and everyone is doing it. That is a lie from the pit of hell. They don't see the correlation between what is going on in their lives is related to the very thing they idolize.

MY ADDICTION

I was in a relationship with someone I had idolized for years, and he was my drug. I know that sounds ridiculous, but it is the truth (truth will set you free). The soul tie between this man and me was profound. Reflecting on those times, I realize he played with my emotions because I often felt like a yo-yo – I could be wound up and dropped at any given time.

After my divorce, I did not heal emotionally before jumping into this relationship. This man had not taken the time to heal or recover from his separation. Notice the wording. We were two broken people trying to find love, a recipe for disaster. When you are empty, and someone comes with smooth-talking words that make you feel good inside, and the dryness you were feeling seems to be gone, those emotions and physical sensations lying dormant begin to stir up. Before you know it, you'll find yourself in a bed of lies and deceit, all for an emotional thrill, the thing we call love, but it isn't.

I was so thirsty for love that I latched on to the first thing that came along. I was not in love. Nor did I have an authentic relationship with this man through the years. I was in bondage. When I was not in his presence, I was lost. And when a song came on the radio, it would take me down memory lane, making me feel good and longing for him even more. Therefore, I urge you to watch what comes across your eye and ear gates. What you allow to enter will influence you.

What begins to happen is that you take all those emotions and rationalize that your actions are okay. You say, "God wants me to be happy." Before you know it, your relationship with God starts to suffer, and you will disconnect yourself from all Godly things.

Many people miss God during these times because, first, they have not saturated themselves with the word of God. Second, they enter into a covenant with people who will be their destruction in the end. When you enter a covenant with someone, you make promises to one another. If that individual you are making promises to is living in darkness, and you are striving to live in the light, it will not work, no matter how much effort you put into the relationship. Let's examine a few scriptures and see why.

- *Ephesians 5:11: "And have no fellowship with the unfruitful works of darkness, but rather reprove them."* You must not entertain the notion of having sexual relationships with anyone who is not your husband. When you connect to something that does not have similar qualities, destruction will follow. You are going one way, and they are going another. Where is the connection?

- *1 Corinthians 15:33: "Be not deceived: evil communications corrupt good manners."* Those who you hang out with will be an indication of who you become. You start to change your values for their values to please them. This includes associates, friends, family members, business partners, or anyone.

Reflecting over those years, I was empty inside but had no clue because so many emotions were present. I thought I would find something to take away the pain. The problem I now see is that he was a temporary bandage to cover up a more significant problem that was going in within me. The devil studies you and knows what you desire, so he repeatedly comes with the same trap. However, we become oblivious to what is happening because we only want our flesh entertained.

I identify with the woman at the well who wanted to be loved and made whole. The problem with this desire is that no other human being can complete you because you are already complete in Christ. God did not create you missing or lacking anything.

I was so addicted to this man that when we would indulge in sexual relations, and it was over, his exact words would be, "I am the devil, and I'm going to take you to hell." WOW -these are some powerful words. The enemy was telling me he was out for my demise. What you speak out of your mouth indicates what is in your heart *(Matthew 12:34).* As clear as day, this man was letting me know what was in his heart. I wasn't listening to him or God.

The enemy will use anyone; most of the time, it will be those closest to you. It is important to watch who you let into your inner circle. After these sexual encounters, I would find myself going down to the altar on Sundays, repenting of my sins. But did that stop me? No. I kept repeating the cycle because I desired him so much.

God saw that I could not shake this man, so he allowed him to call off the relationship (if that's what it was). His exit from my life would not be the last time because he would reenter my life years later, and the process started again. Do I have any regrets? Sure, I do. I regret spending all those years searching for love in another person incapable of loving himself, let alone loving me. We were together for a total of 37 years! Thirty. Seven. Years. Not one time did he bring up marriage. Yet I stayed.

Why are Joseph and Boaz together? Boaz was a protector, provider, observant, compassionate, and, most importantly, a man of integrity. Joseph was hardworking, had a fear of the Lord, could interpret dreams, showed mercy and compassion, and had great patience.

Joseph also was a leader. He showed discipline (Potiphar's wife tried to seduce him) and was faithful, showing incredible loyalty to Potiphar's business, and Potiphar trusted him completely. The best thing about Joseph? He believed in the God he served. I do not doubt that one day God will send that individual who will also have humility, be gracious, and be selfless, and he does not mind helping others in their affairs and assisting me with my purpose and destiny.

Today I am waiting for the man God has for me, with the characteristics of Joseph and my Boaz all wrapped up in one. I know he is out there somewhere.

ADDICTION TO ELECTRONICS & SOCIAL MEDIA

I am talking about an addiction (obsession) to playing video games, watching reality shows on your cell phones 24/7, and having to scroll on Facebook, Instagram, Twitter, and Tik Tok or other social media platforms to see the latest trend.

We can agree that God gave man the knowledge to invent all these gadgets. They are for fun and entertainment. But slowly, the individual is pulled into a world where they start to display a pattern of obsession that becomes risky behavior (like not working). Time goes on, and the individual begins to live out the fantasy. More time goes by, and the game fills that empty void. Now they start to worship that thing, their god (idol). The word idol means an image or representation of a god used as an object of worship.

Both men and women can be addicted to electronics. Some adults spend hours in front of a tv, phone, tablet, or other digital devices. They neglect their families because they are obsessed with living out a fantasy. The word 'fantasy' means "the power or process of creating especially unrealistic or improbable mental images in response to a psychological need." (Merriam-Webster, 2023)

I believe electronic devices and social media applications have subliminal forces (demonic spirits) that subtly infiltrate people's lives but seem innocent. People addicted to these are drawn into a fantasy that they believe benefits them. It is not. Their souls are being systematically sucked dry. They get caught up in the illusion that everything they see is real. As a result, their self-esteem may take a hit. They may think they are 'less than' because their lives don't look like what they see. Don't let that be you.

Addiction to electronics and social media is increasing. Around the world, families are being evicted from their homes because of a lack of responsibility on someone's part. Jobs are lost, or people never even work because of an inability to break free from this. Something is seriously wrong with this picture.

Adults are not the only ones suffering from this addiction. Numerous studies have shown that young children and teenagers sometimes cannot separate their reality from the reality of a game or show. I have seen kids so engrossed in their games that they are oblivious to what is happening around them. What makes this more frightening is that some colleges have introduced gaming curricula. I'm not sure what that entails. I guess you play games all day and get paid for it. Sad.

Researchers show a correlation between spending hours playing games and: a decrease in social skills:

- Neglecting schoolwork
- Increase in weight
- Decrease in good health
- A surge in aggressive behavior

God has given all humankind an imagination. Creative people can bring into the earth's realm what they see in their dreams – a powerful gift if used correctly. But the enemy will hijack people's imagination by building mental scenes that are not real.

What is happening is that they cannot distinguish between reality and fiction. No wonder adults and children are acting out and doing unimaginable things.

Let's talk about reality shows without mentioning any name of a particular show. At one time, I sat and watched these individuals' lives play out on the screen, and I would say, "Boy, they are living large." Everything looked appealing, and I wanted what they had because I was spiritually dehydrated. I was so busy focusing on the things that I missed what was genuinely happening until one day I woke up. I was watching this show, and what I saw began bothering me. Sure, these individuals had everything, but they had so much drama.

Drama sells, but what is it really selling? Is it selling me the reality that dysfunction is okay? If my life is dysfunctional, why watch someone else who is just as dysfunctional or worse off than me? I have enough drama going on in my own life.

Again, trickery and seduction have blinded people. I believe money will make you do anything. Your life is in shambles, and you put your business out for the world to see and judge and offer you advice when the only person you should be seeking advice from is Jesus.

The God we serve is omnipresent and omnipotent. We can always rely on him even when life brings us troubles. The word tells us these things will happen *(John 16:33)*. God says he will intervene and take that desire away. Before you know it, you are free.

"No temptation has overtaken you that is not common to man." 1 Corinthians 10:13

For those of you reading this book, if you are in a crack house, drowning your sorrows with drugs and alcohol, or if you feel that no one cares about you, the Father is waiting on you to cry out to him:

"I love the Lord because he hath heard my voice and supplications. Because he hath inclined his ear unto me, there will I call upon him if I live." Psalm 116:1-2 (NKJV).

MAKING IT PLAIN

How does this relate to soul hydration? When we are addicted to anything but the sweet presence of Jesus, we need soul hydration. In our pursuit to alleviate pain, we create more of what we don't want. Pain.

As women, when we sit for hours on the phone talking to a man who is clearly not going to commit to us, we need soul hydration. When we fall for what I call the okey-doke as I did, our mind has led us to believe this is as good as it gets. Not so!

The Father is eagerly waiting for you to return to Him. There is no judgment about your past or stipulations on what you can have or become in your future. Even if your addictive behavior began long ago, let me share a story.

I shared earlier that I was traumatized as a child because of my dark skin. So, when any boy showed me attention, I gravitated toward him and held on for dear life. That, however, didn't mean that the feeling was mutual.

One boyfriend I had decided to break up with me. Because I was addicted to getting attention, I was not having that. No. He would not break up with me. Do you know what I did? I called the school and told them I decided to die by suicide. I was a child! What did I know or understand about the finality of death? I knew absolutely nothing.

Shortly after I made the call, police officers came to my house and kicked the door in. I was petrified. Not just about having the police in my home. But because I knew my mother would be furious. The officers took me to the hospital. As God would have it, I saw a man who put the fear of God in me.

He explained that I had no idea what I had done. This gentleman also explained that he saw other young girls with many more challenges than I did. He assured me that there would be a lot of other young men in my life. And that what I was threatening to do was not worth it. The thing that got my attention was when he said that all he had to do was sign a piece of paper, and I would be confined to a facility for those with mental health conditions. The prospect of that was overwhelming.

Although this may seem extreme, we all know women who are so empty and parched that they will do almost anything to get the attention they crave. They will even go so far as to threaten to die by suicide. Or they will make a big public spectacle to draw the person back in. Again, soul hydration.

If you, or anyone you know, is in a mental health crisis, dial or text 988. This is the Suicide and Crisis Lifeline. It is available all across the United States at the time of printing this book. When you call, you will be connected to mental health professionals who will connect you to resources during your time of crisis.

THE CHURCH ADDICTION

I can't talk about addiction and not state the obvious for the woman of faith over 50+. She is single, divorced, widowed, or separated. She is the one who is often bypassed in ministry offerings. So she becomes addicted to 'churchin.' What do I mean?

The single, 50+ woman who loves the Lord and is active in her church is vulnerable. Many churches have a Singles Ministry or a ministry for mature church members. However, I believe there is a gap regarding the woman I've described above. One of the most vulnerable times for her is after she has experienced a fantastic worship service and then goes home to an empty house. At that time, she is susceptible to 'Pookie and Bae-bae and nem.'

'Pookie and Bae-bae and nem' will cause you to lose your integrity and compromise your relationship with God. They can lure you further and further away from the Lord. Please don't get caught up in their shenanigans (mischief). 'Pookie and Bae-bae and nem' are not ready to stop living a life out of control. You are not their savior.

Who are 'Pookie and Bae-bae and nem?' These people can be men or women. These are the people who see your vulnerability and will exploit it. Let me give you examples. 'Pookie and Bae-bae and nem' can be:

- a man who has no intention of regarding you as God's daughter with the rights and privileges of royalty.
- a woman who is living a life outside of God's rule, and she consistently wants you to be a part of that.
- a friend (male or female) who does not share your core values about the Kingdom of God and will blatantly disrespect you.
- a person who is fully aware that you have a Kingdom assignment to complete yet offers distraction after distraction to derail you.
- any person who, as our grandmothers would say, "Means you no good."

That's 'Pookie and Bae-bae and nem.'

The enemy of your soul will use them to dehydrate you spiritually. For example, the man I spoke about earlier was a 'Pookie and Bae-bae and nem.' And here's the twist. He would actually go to church with me at times. Or he would come to the service and not let me know he was there. Because our sanctuary is large, I would not see him at all. Later on, in a casual conversation, he would bring up something said in the service or describe something inside of the building. He did this just to let me know he was there.

Looking back, the uncanny thing about this is that he was not trying to use what he learned righteously. He didn't apply the sound doctrine. The sad thing is, I didn't require him to.

My soul was desperate for hydration.

WHAT ABOUT YOU?

Have you ever experienced that 'lonely hour' right after church services? You have just spent a wonderful time fellowshipping with the saints. Now you go to an empty house. You are alone, and you are lonely. The man calls, and the conversation goes like this:

Him: "Hey, beautiful, I was thinking of you. What are you doing?"
You: (Grinning) "Oh, nothing."
Hm: "Would you like some company?"
You: (without hesitation) "Sure."

This man hasn't been a consistent factor in your life at all. He ghosts you (look it up if you don't know what that is). He does not contribute to your emotional well-being. And he most certainly has repeatedly proven that he can come and go in your life whenever he wants. Still, you allow him to come over. One thing leads to another, and you have torn up your Kingdom of God citizen card. :

The same scenario can be played out with a friend:
Them: "What's up?"
You: (Sounding board) "Nothing. What about you?"
Them: "I thought we could (fill in the blank). You want to?"
You: (Without hesitation) "Sure."

You end up participating in an activity that you shouldn't. It doesn't have to be an illegal activity. But it causes you to be distracted and disconnected from God. You know you have a Kingdom assignment to fulfill, and time is of the essence. Instead, you opt for playtime with 'Pookie and Bae-bae and nem.'

Your spiritual dehydration is showing.

SOUL HYDRATING ACTIVITIES

SELF-ASSESSMENT – Addictions

Now that you know addictions come in various forms, take this self-assessment to see how many habits, activities, or people are in your life that you've become addicted to.

This self-assessment is for you. There is no scale, grading, etc. Allow the Holy Spirit to reveal to you the areas he wants you to work on.

1. When I am lonely, I will likely respond positively to attention (in any form).
    a. Always
    b. Sometimes
    c. Never
    d. I need soul hydration.

2. I have people I know are not a good influence in my life.
    a. Always
    b. Sometimes
    c. Never
    d. I need soul hydration.

3. I get bored quickly and turn to food, television, social media, or other things to distract me.
    a. Always
    b. Sometimes
    c. Never
    d. I need soul hydration.

4. I use food to comfort me.
    a. Always
    b. Sometimes
    c. Never
    d. I need soul hydration.

5. I have healthy relationships with myself and others.
    a. Always
    b. Sometimes
    c. Never
    d. I need soul hydration.

6. Have you ever felt you should stop doing an activity or spending time with someone because you began feeling uncomfortable?
    a. Always
    b. Sometimes
    c. Never
    d. I need soul hydration.

7. Have you ever been heartbroken because someone mistreated you but maintained the relationship?
    a. Always
    b. Sometimes
    c. Never
    d. I need soul hydration.

8. Have you allowed others to override what you knew was true in your heart?
    a. Always
    b. Sometimes
    c. Never
    d. I need soul hydration.

9. Have you ever felt guilty after being in someone's presence?
    a. Always
    b. Sometimes
    c. Never
    d. I need soul hydration.

10. Have you ever used a person or activity to soothe your loneliness?
    a. Always
    b. Sometimes
    c. Never
    d. I need soul hydration.

Remember, there is no judgment.

SELAH MOMENT – Addictions

SCRIPTURE FOCUS

The only addiction we should have is to God. Anything else is a substitute for that.

Meditate on the scripture below. Then write down what the Holy Spirit is revealing to you. Think about what is in life (people or activities) that may be setting you up to become an addict – not having control over whether or not you will or won't do something. I've provided additional pages because I know this can be a challenging topic to tackle.

"Don't you realize that you become the slave of whatever you choose to obey? You can be a slave to sin, which leads to death, or you can choose to obey God, which leads to righteous living." Romans 6:16 (NLT)

SELAH MOMENT – Addictions

SELAH MOMENT – Addictions

PART THREE - DELIVERANCE

IT'S FOR YOU

YOU CAN BE SET FREE

Deliverance is possible for anyone suffering from spiritual dehydration and in bondage. It does not matter what type of captivity it is. Let's look at the Samaritan woman.

The Bible does not explain why she had so many men come into her life and leave. It could have been for pleasure, unfulfilled desires, or wanting to entertain her flesh that kept her bound to each man. The Samaritan woman had been beaten down, bruised, and battered by life. She needed to be delivered not only from people but from herself.

And she received her deliverance at the well with Jesus – the Soul Hydrator.

Just as Jesus was waiting for the woman at the well, he is waiting for you. The Father knows what you need when you need it. Forget about your past and what you have done. It will not stop you from experiencing a bright future.

Jesus is no respecter of persons. He delights in showing what he can do with a person others discard. God picks up the despised things that the world disposes of. Man makes up standards for us to try and uphold, but not Jesus.

"But God hath chosen the foolish things of the world to confound the wise; and God hath chosen the weak things of the world to confound the things which are mighty; And base things of the world, and things which are despised, hath God chosen, yea, and things which are not, to bring to naught things that are."
I Corinthians 1:27-28

Every challenge you have been through has prepared you for your assignment for the kingdom. Think about it. How effective can you be if you have yet to go through anything? (If you have no idea what your assignment might be, seek God. He will reveal it to you.)

Before you were in your mother's womb, God created you in his mind and then framed you on his canvas of life. Everything you need to complete the assignment is within you. And many people depend on you to receive deliverance. God was confident that you would reach your destiny and be a catalyst for change for other people.

Your assignment is different from mine. I cannot complete your work, and nor can you complete mine. There are certain people assigned to each of us. Those assigned to you are waiting. They are at an intersection in their life so they, too, can receive deliverance!

To be delivered, you must first recognize that something has you bound. The definition of deliverance has a variety of meanings. All of them mean that God can snatch you from the hands of what has you bound.

Throughout the Bible, we see God (Old Testament) delivering and resecuring his people from all types of danger and Jesus delivering people from all sorts of demonic spirits. In the New Testament, God offers deliverance from sin, evil, death, and judgment. This deliverance is only available through this son Jesus. Let us examine the meanings of the word to be delivered.

The Hebrew word "Natsal (Strong's #5337) defines the word as "to snatch, take away; to snatch out of danger, or to preserve." A good example would be God rescuing his people (Israelites) from the hands of the enemy. Each time God would deliver the children of Israel from the hands of the enemy, they would turn their back on him, yet he still loved them even in their disobedience.

MY DELIVERANCE

Too often, instead of sharing our testimony, we stay close-mouthed for whatever reason, but this is not what God wants us to do. If the Bible is the true compass for our lives, and it is, then we should heed this:

"And they overcame him by the blood of the Lamb, and by the word of their testimony; and they loved not their lives unto the death."
Revelation 12:11

To overcome is to receive deliverance. To help us do that, we must share our story. We already know that the blood of Jesus covers us. But do we know how powerful that combination of the blood and the testimony is? Let me tell you.

I got delivered when I began to talk with other women like me. Women that were guarding a secret with their life, not knowing it was slowly taking their life. My secrets were guilt, shame, condemnation, and despair. I could not let anyone know that I, a woman of God, was dealing with that. Consequently, the enemy had an open door to wreak havoc in my life.

It takes strength and willpower to let go of something you have been holding on to for so long. The word "deliver(s)" is mentioned in the Bible from Genesis to Revelation. Webster defines deliverance as "the action of being rescued or set free; being rescued from bondage or danger."

When people talk about deliverance, what exactly are they referring to? Do you think of "driving" or "calling out" demonic spirits when you think of deliverance? Many people do. Another meaning of deliverance is "to be released from captivity or bondage."

Let me ask you, woman of God (or man of God), what do you need to be released from? I've shared various aspects of my story: challenges, additions, attention-seeking, etc. Are you ready for God to reveal the areas where you must be set free? Have you recognized yourself in the Samaritan woman's story or my story?

God was there the entire time when I was in sin. But one day, I cried out and was snatched from the clutches of the enemy and delivered firmly into the hands of Christ.

When the children of Israel traveled in the wilderness, they found themselves in situations they could not manage. But God would fight for them even in their disobedience. The same is true for you. Our God will not only fight, but he IS also fighting for you right now.

*"For I will deliver the inhabitants of the land unto your hand;
and thou shalt drive them out before thee."
Exodus 23:31*

God has provided many ways to "drive out" your enemy. This book is one way because it exposes the plot against us.

If you must go down to the altar a thousand times for deliverance, Go. Don't be concerned about what people say or think. They don't have a heaven to put you in but can help you go to hell.

JESUS, THE SOUL HYDRATOR

Deliverance is your right, and you need soul hydration to receive it. The only way to get that is through Jesus Christ.

Here is a scripture in various Bible versions to guide you to soul hydration:

"O God, You are my God; early will I seek You; my soul thirsts for You, my flesh faints for You, in a dry and thirsty land with no water." Psalm 63: 1 (MEV)

"God-you're my God! I can't get enough of you! I've worked up such hunger and thirst for God, traveling across dry and weary deserts." Psalm 63:1 (MSG)

"O God of my life, I'm lovesick for you in this weary wilderness. I thirst with the deepest longings to love you more, with cravings in my heart that can't be described. Such yearning grips my soul for you, my God!" Psalm 63:1 (TPT)

"O God, you are my God; earnestly I seek you my soul thirsts for you, my flesh faints for you, as in a dry and weary land where there is no water." Psalm 63:1 (ESV)

*"God, You are my God; I shall be watching for You My soul thirsts for You, my flesh yearns for You, in a dry and exhausted land where there is no water."
Psalm 63:1 (NASB)*

"You, God, are my God, earnestly I seek you; I thirst for you, my whole being longs for you, in a dry and parched land where there is no water." Psalm 63:1 (NIV)

"O God, You are my God; early will I seek You; my soul thirsts for You; My flesh longs for You In a dry and thirsty land Where there is no water." (NKJV)

IT'S JESUS

JESUS COMES ALIVE THROUGH THE BIBLE

Let me show you Jesus through some of the books of the Bible. These excerpts can help you overcome spiritual dehydration by pointing you back to Christ.

MATTHEW: Jesus is our King—point blank, period. As a King, we are his subjects and adhere to Kingdom rule. Jesus, even in his Kingship, experienced everything that you are going through right now. Yes – even every temptation.

"God with us." Isaiah 7:14

Thank God for Jesus, who is with me in all my mess, and because he is with me, I can and will take on any task set before me. I have learned to move out of the way. I had to stop thinking I had everything under control in my power and allow Jesus to be in his role as King over my life. I invite you to do the same.

Jesus is the only one who ever lived in human form and could identify with us as humans and still be God because of the anointing upon his life. Jesus often spoke through parables (short stories illustrating religious or moral principles) to show the truth. Jesus teaches you not to focus on your problems and issues but rather to be concerned about others he leads into your path. Learn to focus on kingdom perspectives and not be self-serving, often leading to destruction. Discover your calling in life and assist Jesus as a kingdom servant.

HEBREWS: Because your soul needs hydration, you may think that no one can understand what you are going through. That is not the case. Meditate upon this:

"For we have not an high priest which cannot be touched with the feeling of our infirmities; but was in all points tempted like as we are, yet without sin. Let us therefore come boldly

unto the throne of grace, that we may obtain mercy, and find grace to help in time of need." Hebrews 4:15

ACTS: This book is a reminder that Jesus is the community leader. Active word – community. You are never alone. Jesus is always with you.

Remember, the early church felt the same stress you feel today. What we learn in our churches on Sundays and Wednesdays allows you to step out on Monday and the rest of the week to face the world's pressures. Again, you are not alone. The continuous coming together of Believers creates a stream where your soul can be hydrated.

"And they continued stedfastly in the apostles' doctrine and fellowship, and in breaking of bread, and in prayers. And fear came upon every soul: and many wonders and signs were done by the apostles. And all that believed were together, and had all things common…." Acts 2:42-44

I CORINTHIANS: This book teaches us about discipleship and many other lessons. Most notably:

"There hath no temptation taken you, but such as is common to man: but God is faithful, who will not suffer you to be tempted above that ye are able; but will with the temptation also make a way to escape, that ye may be able to bear it." I Corinthians 10:13

Read that again. NO TEMPTATION!

Jesus knew you would feel lonely, tired, depressed, etc. But there is a way out. Look for the escape route!

THE LIVING WATER

I'm going to make this plain and simple. Receive your soul hydration now. Get rehydrated in God's presence, his word, and his people.

There are probably thousands and thousands of books out there that speak of the Holy Spirit. No book can contain everything about him.

In conclusion, I want to invite you to receive (or receive again) salvation through repentance and faith.

Receive the Holy Spirit, who will empower and energize you into becoming like Jesus. After Jesus' death and resurrection, he promised to send the Holy Spirit (the Comforter) to be with us in all we do. Jesus said:

"That when the Helper comes, the Spirit of truth, he will bear witness about him."
John 15:26

The moment you receive Jesus into your life, the Holy Spirit takes up residence and is ready to activate every aspect of your life. The Father, the Son, and the Holy Spirit are separate and distinct. Yet they bear witness of the truth.

The Holy Spirit is the spirit of Jesus, revealing to us the truth of the Father's word. The Bible mentions the Holy Spirit many times in the New Testament. Because he is mentioned so many times, this indicates just how important the Holy Spirit is in your life. The purpose of the Holy Spirit is to strengthen you and give you the power you need to walk this life journey.

In the book of Acts, you will read about receiving power when the Holy Spirit comes upon you. This power gives you the ability to witness about Jesus. Life, as I have mentioned in previous chapters of this book, will bring storms and trials. Often you may be tempted to believe you are not to endure them. This erroneous belief is why you need the strength of the Holy Spirit.

One of the things the Holy Spirit does is empower you with the spirit of discernment. The Holy Spirit also guides you in your decisions and protects you even when you don't know you are in danger physically or spiritually. He comforts you and takes away your fears. He refills you with hope.

SOUL HYDRATING ACTIVITIES

SELAH MOMENT – Accepting Deliverance

And *"Call upon me in the day of trouble: I will deliver thee, and thou shalt glorify me." Psalm 50:15*

What you may have done is part of your past.

Don't relive it because you are no longer that person. We all have skeletons in our closet. Your sin is no bigger than my sin. Sin is sin. The moment you accepted Jesus as Lord and Savior, you became a new creature *(2 Corinthians 5:17)*. You are no longer dominated by your sinful nature, and the Holy Spirit now resides within you.

SELAH MOMENT – Practical Steps for Deliverance (Soul Hydration)

You may be wondering about the 'how' of deliverance. Here are some practical steps for deliverance.

It is important to note that I strongly recommend that you consult with your man or woman of God first if you are a member of a faith-based congregation.

Also, know that deliverance is a process. It is not a 'one and done' type of situation. It will take you using these strategies repeatedly – in various areas of your life.

Deliverance Strategies			
If you are:	You may be susceptible to:	Do this	Read this Scripture
Feeling detached, bored, restless	Spirit of loneliness: this will cause you to reach out in unhealthy ways to fill that void.	• Reach out to someone you trust and share what you are going through with them. • Invite people over who are like-minded about living a Kingdom of God lifestyle • Participate in a healthy event or activity that you would not otherwise participate in	For where two or three gather in my name, there am I with them. Matthew 18:20 NIV

Deliverance Strategies			
If you are:	You may be susceptible to:	Do this	Read this Scripture
Wanting to call or connect with someone that you know is not good for you	Soul ties. Simply put – you may have an unhealthy soul tie if you cannot stop thinking about someone or have a persistent desire to be in that person's presence.	• Wait before calling, texting, messaging, or making any other form of contact with this individual. • Ask the Holy Spirit what He would have you to do.	Therefore, I tell you, whatever you ask in prayer, believe that you have received it, and it will be yours. Mark 11:24 ESV
Sexually aroused (for the non-married)	Fornication. In the Christian community, this is when you have sexual relations with someone you are not married to.	• Check what you are watching, reading, listening to, and even the people you are around. • Figure out what triggers you to become sexually aroused.	Put to death, therefore, whatever belongs to your earthly nature: sexual immorality, impurity, lust, evil desires and greed, which is idolatry. Colossians 3:5

Deliverance Strategies			
If you are:	You may be susceptible to:	Do this	Read this Scripture
Mindlessly eating	Sadness or depression. When you are sad or depressed, you may eat without thinking about what, when, or why you are eating.	• Before putting anything in your mouth, check to see if you are truly hungry. • Search for activities, people, events, or circumstances that may trigger mindless eating. • Keep low-calorie (not low-carb) foods around and limit the purchase of unhealthy snacks. • Ask a friend to be an accountability partner to help you keep an eye on your eating.	Then Jesus declared, "I am the bread of life. Whoever comes to me will never go hungry, and whoever believes in me will never be thirsty. John 6:35

Deliverance Strategies			
If you are:	You may be susceptible to:	Do this	Read this Scripture
Feeling abandoned, rejected, discarded, shame, betrayal, guilty (false), or humiliation	Emotional wounds. These events, circumstances, or situations have caused you great pain and anguish that have not been resolved.	• Ask the Holy Spirit for His help • Seek professional help. Yes, you can have Jesus and a therapist too. • Release self-hate, self-unforgiveness, and negative self-talk • Don't expect to heal from an emotional wound quickly. Healing takes time and can be a process	He heals the brokenhearted and binds up their wounds. Psalm 147:3 ESV
Persistent negative self-talk	Word curses and/or strongholds. Word curses are things said to you like, "You'll never be anything." "Why can't you do anything right?" "You are so lazy." Word curses are the complete opposite of a blessing, and they initiate thought strongholds that cause harm to you and death to the plan of God for your life.	•Recognize here a word curse may have taken hold in your life. Speak life. Speak the opposite of the curse over yourself. • Forgive anyone who has spoken a word curse over you. • As much as you can, catch the thought and redirect it while it is 'speaking' to you	You have searched me, LORD, and you know me. You know when I sit and when I rise; you perceive my thoughts from afar." Psalm 139:1 Bless those who persecute you; bless and do not curse them. Romans 12:14 ESV You are altogether beautiful, my darling; there is no flaw in you. Song of Solomon 4:7 ESV

This list of strategies is tiny. I encourage you to use it to address what is happening in your life right now. They all point to a need for soul hydration.

Remember, deliverance is a much broader and deeper topic than what I've addressed here.

I've included some space for you to write out what the Holy Spirit reveals to you regarding areas from which you need deliverance.

SELAH MOMENT – Deliverance Strategies

SELAH MOMENT – Deliverance Strategies

SELAH MOMENT – Deliverance Strategies

SELAH MOMENT – Deliverance Strategies

DRINK AGAIN
(Prayer of Salvation)

I invite you to drink the living water that can only come from Jesus.

Lord, God, forgive me of my sins. Forgive me of any sins that I have committed or any sins of omission. I have been so busy hiding and keeping secrets about my loneliness, depression, sexual activity, etc., that my soul has become dehydrated.

I know that the only thing I need is you. I am a sinner, and I can't save myself. I am coming to you to receive soul hydration. I dedicate (or rededicate) my life to you by faith. By faith, I accept your gift of salvation. I invite you into my life in every area to help me live for you.

I want to drink at the fountain of life that can only be done through you, Lord Jesus. I trust you as my Lord and Savior. Thank you. I believe you are the Son of God. I believe you died for my sins and rose from the dead. Thank you for providing the spiritual nourishment and the living water I need to do your will.

Take over my life right now. In Jesus' name, Amen.

"That if thou shalt confess with thy mouth the Lord Jesus, and shalt believe in thine heart that God hath raised him from the dead, thou shalt be saved."
Romans 10:9

NOW YOU'RE IN THE OVERFLOW & FULLY HYDRATED.

WHAT'S NEXT?

ABOUT DR. LINDA DAY

Linda A. Day is a native of Bronx, New York. After graduating from the New York School System, she entered Talladega College in Talladega, Alabama. She received her Bachelor of Arts in Special Education (with an emphasis in Orientation and Mobility) for the Blind.

After graduating from Talladega College, she entered the United States Armed Forces *(Army)*. Her favorite assignment was Berlin, Germany, and traveling through Checkpoint Charlie into East Germany before the Berlin Wall came down. While stationed in Berlin, she received her Master of Science in Administrative Education from the University of Southern California *(Overseas Program)*.

Dr. Day continued her education by attending Practical Christianity Institute of Evangelism *(PCIE)*-School of Bible Theology Seminary and University, where she received her Masters Level I & II degrees in 2010. In January 2012, she received her Doctorate in Theology from PCIE.

After her active military service, she worked for the Department of Logistics Aviation (formally Defense Supply Center Richmond). While working there, she spearheaded a work-based Bible-study/fellowship group and served as Chaplain for Blacks in Government (BIG). She retired from the Department of Logistics Aviation in 2018.

Dr. Day is a licensed and ordained minister of the Gospel of Jesus Christ. She is a teacher, preacher, and praise dancer. She has traveled abroad to Rajahmundry, India, Uganda, Kenya, and Brazil as a missionary. She has also gone on missionary trips here in the United States. She declares the gospel wherever she goes and worships in spirit and truth. She is a published author. Her first release was *"Single and Sold Out to God."*

Dr. Day loves God's people. Her passion is serving women who are or who were formally incarcerated and those re-entering society from the penal system. Dr. Day served as a minister and teacher under Prison Fellowship for ten years at two federal correctional facilities in Virginia. While there, she became a mentor to numerous women.

Her passion for helping women was the seed for Made In His Image (MIHI). From MIHI, the Faith House International Training Center, Inc. (FHI) was birthed.

Faith House trains individuals in practical occupational skills needed to succeed. FHI provides the tools to assist the incarcerated population in re-entering society and gaining the necessary skills to be successful natural citizens and citizens of the Kingdom of God. The center is a resource to meet all aspects of an individual's needs-spirit, soul, and body.

Dr. Day's motto is: *"You are who you are because you believe in who you can become."* Her favorite scripture is:

"However, I consider my life worth nothing to me, if only I may finish the race and complete the task the Lord Jesus has given men the task of testifying to the gospel of God's grace."
Acts 20:24 (NIV)

Dr. Day is the mother of two adult sons and a grandmother to six. She is a member of Mt. Gilead Full Gospel International Ministries, Richmond, Virginia, under the leadership of Bishop Daniel Robertson, Jr. and Co-Pastor, Elena Robertson.

REFERENCES

Brown, B. (n.d.). *25 Brené Brown Quotes on Vulnerability That Will Change Your Life.* Retrieved from A Thousand Lights: https://athousandlights.com/brene-brown-quotes-on-vulnerability/

Canfield, A. (2016). *THE APOCRYPHAL TWAIN: "THE TWO MOST IMPORTANT DAYS OF YOUR LIFE…".* Retrieved from Mark Twain Studies: https://marktwainstudies.com/the-apocryphal-twain-the-two-most-important-days-of-your-life/

Cleveland Clinic. (2022, November 22). *Why Am I Always Thirsty?* Retrieved from Cleveland Clinic: https://health.clevelandclinic.org/reasons-why-you-may-be-feeling-really-thirsty

Hawkins, R., & Darnell, R. R. (n.d.). *"The Thrill is Gone" Lyrics.* Retrieved from AZLyrics.com: https://www.azlyrics.com/lyrics/bbking/thethrillisgone.html

Hippo, S. A. (n.d.). *Augustine of Hippo - Quotes - Quotable Quote.* Retrieved from Good Reads: https://www.goodreads.com/quotes/73061-to-fall-in-love-with-god-is-the-greatest-romance

M.G. Easton M.A., D. (n.d.). *Samaria.* Retrieved from Bible Study Tools: https://www.biblestudytools.com/dictionaries/eastons-bible-dictionary/samaria.html

Merriam-Webster. (2003). Retrieved from https://www.merriam-webster.com/dictionary/testimony

Merriam-Webster. (2023). *Fantasy.* Retrieved from Merriam-Webster: https://www.merriam-webster.com/dictionary/fantasy

Merriam-Webster. (2023). *Free.* Retrieved from Merriam-Webster Online Dictionary: https://www.merriam-webster.com/dictionary/free

Snyder, K. (2023). *Royal Girlz Ministry.* Retrieved from https://royalgirlz.com/what-is-a-strongman-spirit/

The Britannica Dictionary. (2023). *Idol.* Retrieved from Britannica: https://www.britannica.com/dictionary/idol

What Is A Strongman Spirit. (n.d.). Retrieved from Royal Girlz: https://royalgirlz.com/tag/what-are-the-strongman-spirits/

Wikimedia Foundation. (2023, Aprl 16). *Love of God.* Retrieved from Wikipedia: https://en.wikipedia.org/wiki/Love_of_God

Zacharias, R. (n.d.). *Ravi Zacharias - Quotes - Quotable Quotes.* Retrieved from Good Reads: https://www.goodreads.com/quotes/488026-the-samaritan-woman-grasped-what-he-said-with-fervor-that

Made in the USA
Middletown, DE
04 September 2024

59787297R00066